Senior Parent?

How to Help Your Aging Parents
Live Happy, Healthy Lives;
Without Moving Them to a
Nursing Home, or Moving Them
In With You.

KURT HJELLE

As the owner of my own home care agency (called "Safe at Home Health Care"), I pride myself on providing the highest quality service for seniors and their families.

When I do my first follow-up appointment with a new client and their family, I ask them to fill out a brief survey. It provides great feedback.

Here's the question I ask, along with responses from sixteen of my clients and/or their families:

"If you were going to tell a person who was thinking about using Safe at Home Healthcare, what would you say to him or her?"

"I would highly recommend your agency based on the quality of the caregivers and the supervisor. They had everything set up and working within 24 hours of the initial phone call."
Donald Schutt

"Kurt's engaging and sincere personality set all of us at ease with this very big decision. I give your organization my highest recommendation. Every promise was delivered. It is an agency that provides excellent care with people that have genuine concern for the well-being of their clients."
David Straub

"Could not do better than Safe at Home Healthcare. Loved the personal care. They made me feel very comfortable."
Angela N.

"Our experience has been very good. Having Manuel at the house has been a real life saver."
Barb Reynolds

"We are so happy with the care mom is receiving. Relieved a great deal of stress we were experiencing trying to find the right care for her. Thank you so much for your great agency and the professionalism of your caregiving staff."

Ramona Bosmeny

"Great Service! The caregivers are all great with good attitudes and show caring toward the patient. The owner of the agency is great to work with!"

Aleyna Richardson

"You could not make a better choice. Feel free to use me anytime for a reference."

Nina Whitlock

"I will recommend Safe at Home. I was very happy with the service and would use you again if needed."

Traci Gualano

"We had a good experience with the initial visit, pleased with the information from the website and were very happy with the first impression. Rene just continued to provide such good care, skillful, kind, proactive, anticipated dad's needs. I can't say enough good things about him."

Sheryl Stewart

"This service was recommended to us by one of our friends and we were not disappointed in our choice. We felt all our concerns were answered properly and with understanding."

Charlene Austin

"We would not hesitate to recommend Safe at Home to anyone!"

J. Landis

"We would definitely tell others to use Safe at Home."
B.W Haymond

"Highly rated agency. Good in all aspects"
Mary Jo Devoto

"We have been pleased with Kurt, his agency and the caregivers."
Carol Sluis

"Do it! I appreciate you, Kurt, for checking in frequently."
Laurie Ann Curtin

"Excellent company. Highly recommend."
Brad Luecke

DEDICATION

This book is dedicated to the adult children of our senior citizens.

Helping your parents through the final stages of life is one of the greatest gifts you can give them. It's a demonstration of your unconditional love — the same kind of love they have had for you throughout your entire life.

Life is too short. Cherish every moment, and tell your parents (and your children!) how much you care about them every single day.

TABLE OF CONTENTS

ACKNOWLEDGMENTS

I wouldn't be in the Home Care Agency business if it weren't for Victoria Swan. It was her idea, and I've had the pleasure of working closely with her for many years now.

Many thanks to my wife, Lynn. She has always been supportive of my entrepreneurial endeavors, and my passion for helping seniors and their families.

Why I Wrote This Book

Every single week, I am contacted by a family member — typically the son or daughter of a senior citizen — who is looking for help.

Their parent (or parents) are starting to have some struggles, and it's taking its toll on the entire family.

Here's just a few examples of what your parent might be experiencing:

They might be forgetting to take their medications.

Maybe they aren't bathing frequently or putting on clean clothing each day.

They could be missing meals because meal preparation has become difficult.

Perhaps they're becoming incontinent and they need assistance cleaning up after accidents.

Maybe they've been having issues with balance, or even fallen down once or twice (that they've told you about).

If your parent is having some issues, I'm going to guess that you are stopping by their home frequently - maybe even two or three times per day - to check on them and make sure they are safe.

But eventually it will catch up with you…and on your entire family.

All that time, dedication and assistance can take its toll on all of you.

There are alarming statistics on the impact these additional responsibilities are having on the elderly person's family.

You are being stressed, not just from what you're managing with your parent, but how that time, and possibly, money, is impacting other parts of your life.

I saw an Infographic titled "Exposing the True Costs of a Long Term Care Event," from Genworth, an insurance company that offers long term care insurance.

First, the infographic showed the impact this is having financially on the adult children of senior citizens.

Here's an excerpt:

- they miss an average of 7 hours of work per week
- they lose, on average, 33% of their income for each year they are providing care for their parents
- on average, they spend $10,000 per year on out-of-pocket caregiving expenses
- their savings and retirement funds are being drained to pay for the care of their parent (or parents)

But here's what is worse.

Genworth's data shows that providing care for their parent is also having a huge, negative impact on their own personal health.

- 54% experience negative feelings as a result of providing care, including guilt and resentment.
- 43% said it negatively affected their personal health and well-being.
- 51% said providing care for their parent reduced the time they spent with their children, spouses/partners, or time taking care of themselves.

I could go on and on with data and information - but here's what is important.

There are all kinds of experts who can help you through this time — you simply need to connect and seek out their help.

There are attorneys; doctors; insurance companies; both home care agencies and home health care agencies that specialize in issues for elder care; and home care mentors (a program I'll explain to you later), to name a few.

There is a lot of information — possibly too much information — from many different sources. (Don't worry - this book will guide you through all of it.)

It can be confusing and overwhelming to navigate through it all, and make good decisions.

Plus, you might have several family members involved in caring for and making decisions for your seniors, and that's a good thing. But it can also make decision-making more difficult, depending on your family dynamics. That's when independent third-parties can be especially helpful.

I've assembled the information in this book to be your step-by-step guide for every aspect of assisting an aging parent.

It will take you through what to do at each phase of your parent's transition from experiencing a few issues, to, hopefully many years down the road, when they have passed.

Most seniors would prefer to remain in their own home as long as possible (and as long as they have assistance, many can stay in their homes for several years).

What's most important is their safety and security.

If you've been given this book as a gift, or you've found it in a professional's office, please be sure to check out the back cover.

You'll find contact information for a team of professionals in your area to contact for various services.

If you found this book online, my team of "mentors" and I will be happy to help you connect with the best professionals in your area.

As the name "mentor" implies, they are an independent third party who is committed to making sure your parent gets the level of service they need — and at the same time, they aren't "over-sold" services that aren't necessary at this time.

There is absolutely no charge to you for their services, and I strongly recommend using Home Care Mentor's services. It will give you confidence in your decisions.

Here's what's most important. We all have a common goal. We want your parent(s) to be happy, healthy and safe — and truly enjoy the final years of their lives.

Kurt Hjelle

How to Use this Book

This book is intended to help you navigate through the important actions and decisions you need to make, as your parents, or another special senior in your life, start their transition to the end of life.

This is important: The sooner you take care of many of these things — especially before your parent is having any issues — the better it is for your entire family.

Many of the items you'll learn about can help protect your parents' finances and assets.

Discussing and knowing your parents' wishes, when they may not be able to make those decisions for themselves, can prevent stern discussions, even arguments between you and your siblings at a time when emotions are already running high.

Plus, you'll be well-informed, and you'll be connected to people who are experts in providing the services you and your family members may eventually need.

Read through the entire book, and take advantage of all the checklists and evaluations.

I've got several resources for you, including my special "Should Your Parent Be Living Alone" quiz, and my "Checklists Packet" - which are incredibly helpful.

Go to: SafeatHomeHealthCare.com

If you were given a copy of this book by a professional service provider, you will also find a list of contact information for professionals in each category of service in your area, inside the back cover of this book.

If you ordered this book online, feel free to reach out so I can connect you with professionals that my team and I have personally screened in your area.

Finally, keep this book handy so you can access the information as a refresher at times when you're making decisions about every "next step" for the seniors in your life.

It's intended to be a long-term reference.

Part One - Introduction

<u>Safety First</u>

Hopefully your parents live long, healthy lives. But for most, as they age, they can experience many different challenges - both physically and mentally.

The most important criteria in every decision you make is to keep your Senior safe.

That means choosing housing and, if necessary, home care assistance, that will support both their physical and mental health.

<u>Housing Options</u>

Let's face it. All of us would like to live a long, healthy life.

We want to remain active, keep our independence (especially when it comes to driving or getting around), continue to live the lifestyle that we're accustomed to, and stay in our own homes until we pass away one night in our sleep.

But most often, that is not the case.

Here's a list of various housing options for Seniors (I will be covering them in-depth later in the book.)

1)   The Senior remains in their own home, and use home care services, provided by a well-trained, compassionate caregiver.
2)   The Senior remains in their own home, and uses home health care services, provided by a nurse or other licensed health care professional.
3)   Living with one of their adult children, or another relative.

4)   Assisted living facility.
5)   Nursing home care.
6)   Hospice.

Obviously you have lots of choices and decisions to make as your Senior's needs change. These can become emotional situations, and family dynamics can complicate things even more.

That's why I always encourage families to do so much preplanning.

I've been helping seniors and their families for nearly 20 years, and I know how difficult this process can be for the entire family.

It's what inspired me to develop a unique FREE service to families that I call "Home Care Mentors."

I have personally trained compassionate individuals how to connect with families (either in-person, by phone, or even virtually), become acutely aware (using assessments and checklists) of your Senior's level of need, and then make recommendations for services and help you connect with professionals in your area.

(I'll explain more about this later. Just know that these are independent third parties who can help you wade through all of the factors involved, and make good decisions.)

You and your Senior are not charged a fee. (For more information, go to **SafeatHomeHealthCare.com**)

Having "The Talk" With Your Parent(s)

No one likes to talk about their death.

Family dynamics, which can be difficult, often enter into the picture.

The fact is — people — including you — should plan appropriately for their elder years — earlier, not later.

Think about it. AARP (The American Association of Retired Persons) offers its memberships starting at age 50. Why wait until your Senior is in their '70s or '80s to plan well?

People and families who plan ahead can:
- Protect and preserve assets for themselves and their children.
- Maintain their independence and choice.
- Ensure they receive quality care.
- Make sure they don't become a burden to their family members.
- Prevent being impoverished and dependent on Medicaid.
- Should they experience a debilitating event, ensures their wishes for care (for example, not being kept alive on machines) are met.

As difficult as it might be, ask your Seniors if you can sit down to review their elder care plan.

Explain that your only goal is to be able to carry out their wishes, in the unlikely event they can't make those decisions themselves.

Use the information and checklists in this book, and connect with the professionals in your area, listed inside the back cover (or reach out for assistance from my team and me by going to **SafeatHomeHealthCare.com**).

At the same time you go through this process with your Parents, proceed with similar planning for yourself.

The Biggest Reason to Start Planning Early

I can sum it up in one single word: **MONEY**

Long term care is expensive. Early financial planning can mean having many more options when it comes to long term care.

The cost of care looks like this:

According to the data from Genworth Long Term Care Insurance Company:

- The national average daily rate for a private room in a nursing home is $253/day or $92,345 annually.
- The national average daily rate for a semi-private room in a nursing home is $225 or $82,125 annually.
- The national average hourly rate for home health aides is $22/hr. For only 5 hours of care 7 days per week, the monthly average cost is $3,080 per month or $36,960 annually.

Privately paying for long-term care means that seniors would have to find an additional $36,960 to $92,345 per year in their budget for just ONE person to receive care.

Most of us, seniors or not, could not afford to privately pay for our own care year after year.

Let me make it clear — I'm not a financial planner, and I'm not trying to give you any kind of financial advice. (That's why it's so important to connect with professionals NOW.)

The good news about these costs: there are many ways to plan ahead and manage your finances now, so paying for long term care is never an issue. (I'll explain some of the options in future sections.)

Just like what you learned many years ago about savings accounts; the longer time you have to invest in different financial planning tools — such as long term care insurance — the more money you'll have available when you need it.

Betty's Story...an example of unexpected need for home care and other services.

I first met Betty when she contacted my Home Care Agency (Safe at Home Health Care) for help with home care for her husband, Paul.

He was battling cancer, and Betty was providing all of his care, but she needed a surgical procedure herself, so they needed assistance while Betty recovered.

My home care agency provided home care services for her husband — preparing his meals, and assisting him with personal hygiene and medications — especially since he had some signs of mild dementia.

After Betty recovered from her procedure, she was able to take on Paul's care again. Paul eventually passed away.

A couple years later, Betty took her family on a trip to Hawaii, and they had a great time. I'm sure it included sharing great memories of Paul - husband, father, and grandfather.

But just a week or two after they got home from the trip, Betty had a stroke - a totally unexpected event.

Mentally Betty was fine. But she was having some difficulty with her speech. She also had right arm and right leg paralysis.

She was transferred from the hospital to a rehab facility where she spent five months working to regain her mobility.

Betty worked hard in rehab and improved to a level where she needed only minimal assistance. Specifically, at this stage, she needed assistance with transfers (going from a bed to a chair, etc.), activities of daily living such as using the restroom, bathing, grooming, dressing, and walking with assistance (to prevent a fall).

Betty wanted to go home. She wanted to sleep in her own bed. She didn't want to go into assisted living or a nursing home. She wanted to maintain her personal routines and freedoms.

So my agency set-up a home caregiver to assist her with her non health-care needs.

But Betty also needed services that required a licensed health care professional — physical therapy, speech therapy, and occupational therapy.

The nursing home (where she stayed for her rehab) made arrangements for a nurse to come to Betty's home. (This is called home health care services.)

I inspected their home, and I found she needed to make some changes to facilitate her new lifestyle (remember - our main goal is to make sure they are safe).

Betty and her family had to change the restroom to allow room for a wheelchair, including installation of a different tub/shower, adding a tub-transfer bench, and purchasing a bedside commode (which can also fit over the toilet).

Once the alterations were complete in her home, and all of her service providers were in-place, Betty moved back home. She got her wish.

These days Betty is happy, safe at home with a private caregiver, and her adult children have peace of mind and liberty knowing their Mom is OK at home. They can be working or enjoying their grandchildren, knowing someone is watching over Betty, and that caregiver will call them if they are needed for anything.

A sudden event (Betty's stroke), and she went from hospital, to rehab, then transitioned back home with the assistance of both home care and home health care services.

This is an example of how living requirements and care needs can change — often rapidly — for your Senior.

Fortunately, Betty and her husband had planned well financially. She had the financial resources, which allowed her to make choices.

That's why it's so important to meet with professionals and plan well now.

Part Two: Advance Planning

As I explained in the previous section, the earlier your Seniors plan for their future care, the better.

There are four key areas to address:

Legal issues, insurance, financial planning, and funeral planning.

I strongly recommend that you meet with a local expert (if you don't find a name and contact information in the back cover of this book, contact my team and me through my website: **SafeatHomeHealthCare.com**).

Regulations and products will vary from state-to-state, which makes using the services of local professionals critically important.

In the next section, I'm going to review each area and give you an initial checklist of items to discuss with each professional. It's quite possible this list is not all-inclusive, but it gives you a place to start.

A. Legal

One of the very best gifts parents can give to their children is to leave their affairs in good order. It also ensures that their wishes and desires are carried out upon their death.

Aging adults and their family members face challenging legal issues. These can be complicated for both the Seniors, and their adult children. That's why it's critically important to choose an attorney who specializes in dealing with these issues.

Specifically, when you choose an attorney, make sure he/she is an attorney who specializes in *elder law.*

Meeting Preparation

The first step to be well prepared for a meeting with an attorney is to gather all of your Senior's important documents. (Download my "checklist packet" at **SafeatHomeHealthCare.com**.)

Not only will this make the meeting easier, but it can save you in fees, since attorneys typically charge based on time.

Organize the documents and keep them in a safe place — in a fireproof locked box, or in a safe-deposit box at a bank.

Decide who should have access to the information, and give each of those persons a key.

Legal issues and financial issues often overlap, so it's better to bring all of your documents to your meetings with an attorney.

Your attorney might need to connect with your financial advisors, so be sure to have his/her contact information available.

Topics to review with an Elder Law Attorney:

1) Estate Planning

Estate planning means you prepare for the transfer of a person's wealth and assets after his or her death. Assets, life insurance, pensions, real estate, cars, personal belongings and debt are all part of your Senior's estate.

Your attorney might recommend using tools such as trusts and life estates to protect your Senior's assets.

With a **trust,** property is held by one party for the benefit of another. The trustee holds that property for the trust's beneficiaries.

With a **life estate**, ownership of property is transferred immediately upon death to your Senior's beneficiary, but until that time, the Senior maintains ownership benefits.

Like I explained, these can be complicated issues. A good Elder Law attorney will determine the best options for your Senior's circumstances, and explain all the details.

2) Guardianship (a.k.a. Conservator — the name varies from state-to-state)

This is used for adults who become incapable of making responsible decisions, due to a mental disability or deterioration (such as dementia).

The guardian can be authorized to make legal, financial, and health care decisions for the Senior.

Typically, this is the type of client that is assigned a Geriatric care manager by a trust officer or attorney. Geriatric Care Managers are licensed health care professionals who also become the Senior's Guardian, and can make all of the Senior's legal, financial and health care decisions.

3) Power of Attorney

This document gives a person (called agent or attorney-in-fact) the authorization or permission to act on your behalf in legal and financial matters.

Power of Attorney can be limited to a single transaction, or it can be "durable" power of attorney, which gives the agent the power to do almost anything your Senior could do.

This does not have to be one the senior's adult children.

Sometimes, depending on how well your family gets along, it can be difficult for a Senior to choose just one of their adult children to act as your Power of Attorney.

Here's an example:

Recently my agency provided home care services for Jim and Barbara, a married couple.

Jim could no longer take care of Barbara because he was suffering from severe low back pain.

When he first asked me to come over to their home for an assessment meeting - I arrived at their home to meet a woman named Susan, who I assumed was Jim's and Barbara's daughter. It turned out Susan was an RN. Because their 3 children did not get along, they made the decision to appoint Susan — a trusted third-party — as their Power of Attorney - both for health care and finances.

Obviously you have to trust that person tremendously.

If, for whatever reason, you do not want to assign Power of Attorney to one of your adult children or other family members, consider a trusted third-party who can look at things objectively and not be emotionally attached to the situation, as a son or daughter, or loved one might be.

In some cases, a geriatric care manager can be appointed as your Power of Attorney. (You'll find more information about what a Geriatric Care Manager does in an upcoming chapter.)

4) Advance Directive - Power Attorney of Healthcare

If your Senior has some type of medical event or accident that has left them unconscious or too ill to communicate, the advance directive will take any guessing out of your decision-making process.

If their heart stops, do they want to be resuscitated? Do they want to live on breathing machines?

Hopefully you and your family never has to make these difficult decisions — but if you do, with an advance directive, you'll know exactly what your Senior wants you to do.

I have a very personal story that stresses the importance of working with an attorney for the types of legal work I just described...

My in-laws, Joan and John, never talked about advanced directives.

They, like a lot of seniors, didn't want to talk about death, because they thought, "If we talk about it, it will happen tomorrow."

That's not the best thinking or approach.

It was just after election day in 2004. My father-in-law was a Democrat, and my mother-in-law is a Republican. I'm sure you can imagine the "heated discussions" we often witnessed at the dinner table.

I called Joan to congratulate her on the election results, since her candidate, President Bush, won.

As we were talking on the phone. She suddenly heard a bang, and said to me, I think your Father-in-law just fell upstairs. I told her she better hang up and go check.

Sure enough, he had fallen, and it caused internal bleeding. John was rushed to the hospital.

After further examination, he had severe internal bleeding going on, and my Mother-in-law had to make the decision, while her husband was unconscious, of not taking any life saving measures.

Within 5 hours he passed away.

She had to make difficult decisions because nothing was in place.

5) Financial Power of Attorney

This is similar to a "Power of Attorney," but it is strictly limited to acting on the Senior's behalf in financial matters.

6) Living Will

A *living will* is one type of advance directive to be used when your Senior can no longer express informed consent. It is a written document, and it would be shared with hospital staff.

As I stated earlier, I'm not an attorney. Your Senior may have additional issues specific to your state or your family's situation.

I'm not intending to give you legal advice. I'm simply giving you information to help you prepare for a meeting with an Elder Law Attorney.

I've seen and talked to many other families who don't have living wills or power of attorney in place.

Sit down with your parents. Meet with the Elder Law Attorney or Estate Planning Attorney to talk about the future.

Do it this week, or this month. Don't delay.

Insurance

Often when we think about insurance, we think about insuring our cars, our homes, and our belongings, in case of some type of accident, theft, or fire.

We also think about health insurance, to cover most or all of our medical expenses; and life insurance to provide for our families after we pass.

A type of insurance, that can be a great financial planning tool, is ***long term care insurance.***

The term "long term care" covers a wide range of your Senior's needs.

It can include paying for a home caregiver to provide assistance with daily activities, such as eating and dressing, and health monitoring. It might pay for adult day care. And, it might cover all or partial expenses for our Senior's residency in an assisted living facility or nursing home.

This is important. The services I just listed *are not* typically covered by regular health insurance or Medicare. Medicaid may cover some of these costs, but only to those with very limited financial resources.

The good news is these services can be paid for with long term care insurance benefits.

I'm not in the insurance business myself, and long term care insurance products vary from company-to-company, and from state-to-state.

Please connect with the insurance agent whose name is inside the back cover of this book - or go to my website for more information and my team and I can help you connect with an insurance professional in your area. Go to: SafeatHomeHealthCare.com.

Here are the **five biggest reasons your Senior should consider investing in long term care insurance**:

1) Independence.

It's better to be in a financial position to make choices about care and residency, rather than needing to rely on family members.

2) Protect your assets.

Whether you're protecting your assets for your spouse's sake, or you want to leave your children with an inheritance, long term care insurance can offset the high costs of long term care.

3) Affordability.

Long term care services are expensive. It's much easier to make decisions about the best home care or adult day care services for your Senior when you aren't stressed about the financial aspects.

4) Options.

With the protection of long term care insurance, your Senior can make choices beyond nursing home care. Plus, this insurance may cover the costs of nursing home care, if needed.

5) Standard of living.

It's the reason most seniors want to stay in their own homes as long as possible, or live in assisted living to enjoy the social aspects of those facilities. They want to live out their final years enjoying the same kind of lifestyle they are accustomed to living.

There are a wide variety of long term care policies. These are some of the features to discuss with your insurance provider (from the Agis website):

Coverage. A policy may be limited to a certain type of location, such as your home or a nursing facility. Many policies cover a range of options, including assisted living, adult day care, and even care provided by a family member or friend.

Benefit triggers. In a typical policy, benefits begin when you can no longer perform at least two activities of daily living (such as bathing and eating) without help. Before buying a particular policy, make sure you understand the triggers.

Benefit limits. When the cost of care exceeds your daily or monthly benefit, you must pay the remaining balance. A policy may also have limits on your total benefits in terms of both time and money. Make sure you understand the details. Some policies have separate maximums for different types of care.

Elimination or waiting period. During this period, you must pay all of your long-term care expenses. The shorter the waiting period, the higher your premiums. Make sure your Senior understands that they need to save enough money to fulfill the requirements of the elimination period. (The elimination period is the number of days, during which the insurance company is not responsible for expenses.)

Inflation protection. As health care costs continue to rise, inflation protection becomes essential. The two main types of inflation protection are automatic coverage increases and the right to add coverage later. In other words, with inflation protection, your policy should cover the cost of care — whether it's at today's rates, or rates that have increased over time, due to inflation.

Non-forfeiture benefit. A policy with this feature may provide coverage even if you're unable to continue paying premiums.

Ask your insurance agent to review and explain every benefit of a long term care product, to ensure you will be investing in the coverage you need.

Your insurance professional should be willing to answer all of your family's questions— and should understand the long term care industry and insurance products thoroughly.

One final note: the earlier in life your Senior invests in a long term care insurance product, the more benefits/protection they will have when they need it.

Financial

Every person should work with a financial planner, no matter what the size of your "nest egg."

A financial planner has the knowledge to evaluate your overall financial picture, and make recommendations to help you get the best returns on your financial resources.

(Look for the name of your local Financial Planner in the back cover of this book, or go to my website for assistance - **SafeatHomeHealthCare.com**.)

In addition to assistance with managing 401K accounts, IRAs, SEPP-IRAs, and investments; if your Senior needs additional financial resources, your Financial Planner can make recommendations that are best for your overall financial picture.

Let me give you an example:

So many of my clients want to be able to stay in their homes. But often they might not have the financial resources to pay for home care services.

One financial strategy that can help you accomplish both goals — keeping your Senior in their home, and providing home care services to keep them safe — is a "reverse mortgage."

Most seniors have either paid off the mortgage on their homes, or they have a significant amount of equity in their homes. A "reverse mortgage" is a loan against that equity, and the proceeds can be used for any purpose.

To qualify, your Senior must be at least 62-years-old, they must live in their home as their primary residence, and they must have equity in their home.

There are no income or medical qualifications. Disbursements are tax-free and can either be received as a lump sum, as a monthly payment, as a line of credit, or combination of all three methods. (That's why it's called "reverse mortgage" - the lender pays your Senior, rather than your Senior paying the bank - so they are tapping into the equity of their home without having to sell or move.)

When your Senior moves, or passes away, the loan must be repaid.

That's just one example of some of the creative financial solutions you can learn about by working with a financial planner.

Government Assistance Programs

Individuals

If your Senior doesn't have the personal financial resources to cover the cost of any of the services described above, you need to connect with their state agencies to determine what programs are available.

These vary from state-to-state, and change frequently.

TIP!

Search google for "health and human services YOUR STATE" to easily find its website.

Sadly, your Senior won't have as many choices as those who have prepared financially, but what is most important is to get your Senior the very best care possible.

Veterans

I am so grateful every single day for the men and women who serve in our military. Before I jump into the benefits available for Veterans, please thank your Senior, from my team and me, for serving our country.

To get the full list of requirements, you can contact your local Veteran's Administration office or go to our Resource section of the book for an Elder Law Attorney.

The Veteran, Widowed Spouse, and Dependent or Disabled Children can receive benefits.

Here's a recent list of requirements (and this is included in my special checklist packet, available at **SafeatHomeHealthCare.com**):

- Veteran must have served at least ninety days active duty with one day of the ninety during a qualified war period (ninety days must generally be consecutive, with some exceptions)
- Veteran must have had an other than "dishonorable" discharge
- Claimant's physician must declare him/her as in need of assistance from another individual, which may include services offered by assisted living.
- Claimant should have limited household assets; excluding their primary home, car, and personal belongings. If assets are jointly owned by someone other than the spouse, only the claimant's share is generally countable. In the case of a married veteran, the couple's combined assets are countable.
- There is no longer a current asset cap, per se. The VA now considers the claimant's life expectancy in determining how much a claimant can have. In the case of assets over $50k, it may be best to consult an elder law attorney. Transferring assets without the proper legal / professional advice is strongly discouraged.
- Claimant's household out-of-pocket yearly medical expenses must exceed or come close to his / her total yearly household gross income (total yearly cost of assisted living is typically considered a medical expense)
- Widowed spouse must have been married to the veteran for at least one year OR have had children

by the veteran if married less than one year and never remarried (with possibly one very rare exception).

- Widowed spouse must have been living with the veteran at the time of the veteran's death, unless the separation was due to medical or military reasons (there may be some exceptions made related to separations due to abuse).
- Minor or disabled adult children may qualify for limited benefits on their own.

Pre-Planning Their Funeral

I know, most Seniors (or anybody for that matter) don't want to think about what happens when they die.

But here are some reasons for connecting with a local mortician to pre-plan your funeral:

1) It will ease the burden on you and your other family members, so you don't have to make difficult decisions during this trying time.

For example - do you know if your Senior wants to be buried or cremated? Will they prefer an open or closed casket? What type of funeral ceremony do they prefer? If they want to be buried, where? What kind of headstone do they prefer?

Pre-planning ensures that your Senior's final wishes are followed.

2) A funeral can be pre-paid, so your Senior will not leave their heirs with a financial burden.

There are funeral insurance products, or funeral trusts that can be used to plan for the costs of your Senior's funeral.

3) Pre-planning gives you the benefit of a meaningful funeral. It's important in the grieving process, and will give you a sense of closure. It also will give you and your family members the ability to start the healing process.

4) Your Senior will leave their affairs in order at the end of their life. They can spend their final days without concern or worry.

(Please see the name and contact information for your local funeral home and mortician in the back cover of this book, or by going to my website at:
SafeatHomeHealthCare.com.)

Part Three:

When Your Senior's Health or Mobility Starts to Deteriorate - How to Keep Your Parent Safe in their Home

In most cases, changes in your Senior's health, or ease in moving around the house, happen slowly over time.

Plus, you probably visit them often, so you may not notice changes.

It's important to watch for some key signs that your Senior may start to need some assistance with daily tasks.

Falls

- Is your Senior stumbling or falling down?

- Are you noticing any bruising that might indicate they have fallen, but have not told anyone?

- Or worse, have they experienced a fall that required a visit to the emergency room or hospital?

Not taking their medications, as prescribed

- Helping your Senior prepare their medications using plastic pill boxes can help you monitor their consumption.

- If there are pills left in the container that they forgot to take, or if they are running out of medications prior to their refill dates, you know there are issues.

Personal hygiene

- As activities such as bathing, dressing, or even doing the laundry regularly, become difficult; you might notice that your Senior does not keep up on their personal hygiene.

- Pay attention to the clothes they are wearing during each visit. If your Senior is wearing the same clothing frequently, they may be having difficulty dressing and undressing.

- Does their hair appear clean and recently washed? If not, they could have issues getting in and out of a tub or shower.

- Check their undergarments. Are they having problems with incontinence or soiling?

Food

- Consider taking your Senior to the grocery store to observe what they purchase.

- Look in the refrigerator to see if food is spoiling, and to monitor leftovers.

- If your Senior is having issues in any of these areas, its an indication that they are in need of an evaluation, and possibly some assistance.

My Team and I Want to Help

My company offers a free service, called **"Home Care Mentors,"** that I created to help Seniors and their families.

Let's face it. Family dynamics can be difficult - especially when you're dealing with the safety and well-being of your parents.

A **Home Care Mentor** is a compassionate individual that I have personally trained.

They will connect with and your Senior to evaluate whether or not your Senior needs additional care, and can make recommendations for home care or other types of services, if needed.

They are just as the name implies: **a Mentor**

Home Care Mentors are independent third parties who strictly want to help families keep their Seniors safe and happy as they progress through their final stages in life.

This is a FREE service.

Look for the name and contact information for a Home Care Mentor in your area on the back cover of this book, or connect with my team and me by going to **SafeatHomeHealthCare.com.**

Should Your Senior Live Alone in their Home?

I use several evaluation tools that can help you evaluate whether or not your Senior can continue to live by themselves in their home.

The first step in their evaluation is to review any issues your Senior is experiencing.

Here's the information (you will find this in the forms packet at SafeatHomeHealthCare.com and a Home Care Mentor can also help you review this entire list).

EVALUATION: Should Your Relative Live Alone?

SAFETY NEEDS

☐ YES ☐ NO Has your relative had accidents because of weakness, dizziness or inability to get around?

☐ YES ☐ NO Has the use of the stove, oven or appliances become a safety problem because of forgetfulness?

☐ YES ☐ NO Are there hazardous conditions in his/her home, such as the bathroom or bedroom being on separate floors? Have stairs become an obstacle?

☐ YES ☐ NO Does your relative refuse to use a wheelchair, walker, or other assistive devises necessary for safety and therefore is at risk for falling?

☐ YES ☐ NO Does your relative express a desire to die, or seem to be depressed, apathetic or without an interest in living?

NUTRITIONAL NEEDS

☐ YES ☐ NO Is there a demonstrated nutritional problem (i.e. weight loss, illness, anemia?)

☐ YES ☐ NO Does your relative eat only inappropriate foods that will not supply nutritional needs?

☐ YES ☐ NO Does your relative "forget" to eat?

PERSONAL NEEDS

☐ YES ☐ NO Is your relative unable to get to the toilet when necessary?

☐ YES ☐ NO Is your relative unable to change clothing or bed linens as necessary to remain clean & dry?

☐ YES ☐ NO Are they able to do laundry and housework?

MEDICAL NEEDS

☐ YES ☐ NO Does your relative forget to take necessary medications?

☐ YES ☐ NO Is it likely that your relative would take an inappropriate does of medicine purposely or accidentally?

☐ YES ☐ NO Is your relative physically unable to handle medications (spills or drops them) or to give injections?

☐ YES ☐ NO Is your relative unable to obtain help in case of need?

SOCIAL NEEDS

☐ YES ☐ NO Is your relative unable to handle money?

☐ YES ☐ NO Does your relative get lost in familiar situations?

☐ YES ☐ NO Has your relative left home without a destination?

☐ YES ☐ NO Does your relative often behave inappropriately?

☐ YES ☐ NO Does your relative have mental or emotional problems which might be a threat to self or others?

If you answered **"YES"** to 5-to-9 of these questions, you should be thinking of, and planning for, the probability that your relative will need additional care and support in the future.

It might be time to think about completing a Power of Attorney for Finances and Health Care for the future decision making events (if you haven't already put those in place).

If you answered, **"YES"** to 10 or more of these questions, support services are very likely needed immediately. Your Home Care Mentor can help you connect with a home care agency that they have personally reviewed.

Next - Conduct a Home Assessment

(This form is also in the forms packet at
SafeatHomeHealthCare.com, and a Home Care Mentor can
help you and your Senior with this evaluation.)

Check any of the following items that present problems.
Please use this as a guide to help locate problem areas in
your Senior's home:

Entry

____ Climbing the stairs to the front door
____ Going down the stairs from the front door
____ Unlocking the front door
____ Using the door knob
____ Reaching and using the mailbox
____ Walking over the lip at the threshold
____ Adequate lighting
____ Other obstacles
____ Two forms of egress

Hallways and Inside Doors

____ Opening and going through doors to rooms
____ Using door knobs
____ Moving between carpeted and non-carpeted areas
____ Adequate lighting
____ Turning on lights in the area being approached

Stairs

___ Slipping on stairs
___ Distinguishing the thresholds and edges
___ Tracking over bare treads or other obstacles
___ Balancing, support

Kitchen

___ Turing lights on and off
___ Using electrical outlets
___ Opening and closing windows
___ Adequate lighting
___ Using cabinets, closets, and other storage
___ Using and reaching all parts of the refrigerator/freezer
___ Using counters or other surfaces (preparing meals)
___ Using the oven (door, dials, shelves)
___ Reaching the switch on the range fan
___ Using the stove (dials, reaching the burners)
___ Using water taps
___ Cleaning the floor and other surfaces
___ Using the dishwasher
___ Disposing trash/garbage

Bathroom

____ Entering and exiting

____ Privacy

____ Turning lights on and off

____ Using electrical outlets

____ Using cabinets and closets

____ Using the mirror

____ Using water taps

____ Using the sink

____ Using the toilet

____ Using the shower/bathtub

____ Adequate lighting

____ Opening and closing the window

Managing Your Senior's Medications

Monitoring all of your Senior's prescriptions and medications to ensure that he/she is either taking them as directed, or not taking more than prescribed is critically important.

As explained earlier, using a plastic 7-day or 28-day pill box (available at any drug store) can help your Senior manage their medications, and help you monitor their consumption.

In addition, I recommend setting up a "Vial of Life" system.

Vial of Life

The Vial of Life is simply this: a brief information sheet including current medications, allergies, doctor's names, next of kin etc. is placed in a vial (which can be a blank prescription drug container, or any small bottle or container of any kind) .

The Vial is then placed inside the refrigerator on the door, or in the freezer.
A magnet or sticker is then placed on the front door (on the inside) alerting emergency medical personnel that vital information is located in the refrigerator.

Most EMS personnel are trained to look for the vial of life or some indication that vital information is easily accessible in the house.

You can contact your local fire department to see if they have Vial of Life or File for Life kits that contain the form, vial, and stickers. (Your Home Care Mentor can assist you with creating your Senior's Vial of Life, or download it **SafeatHomeHealthCare.com**)

A third option is a new, online system called Smart 911 (www.Smart911.com).

Smart911 is a free service used by public safety agencies across the country to enhance communication and response for their community. It can be used by 9-1-1 agencies to quickly send first responders to the location of an emergency with more information, by emergency management to better plan for and respond to disasters, and by municipalities to send emergency notifications to their citizens.

By creating a Safety Profile for your family, you are providing potentially life- saving information to public safety officials at the time when they need it most.

Today over 70% of calls made to 9-1-1 in the U.S. are made from mobile phones, and these mobile phones relay limited information about the caller.

Unlike a landline, a mobile phone does not link directly to an address or include a caller's name. 9-1-1 call takers are trained to ask specific questions to determine the location of the emergency, who is in need of assistance and other specific details in order to send the correct response teams, to the correct location, quickly. These questions take time, and often during an emergency the caller may not be able to communicate effectively. By creating a Smart911 profile the call taker will have all the information they need to help you quickly.

58 Ways to Make Sure Seniors are Safe at Home

Based on nearly 30 years of working with Seniors and their families, I've learned that there are many things you should do - things you may not be thinking about — to keep your Seniors safe in their homes.

This will also help you sleep better at night, knowing that your Senior is not going to be in danger.

Here's my list. (This is also in the forms packet at **SafeatHomeHealthCare.**com and can be reviewed with your Home Care Mentor.)

Note: This information is not meant as medical advice, nor is it all-inclusive.

The List: 58 Ways to Make Sure Seniors are Safe at Home

COMMUNICATION:

1. Emergency telephone numbers for the Police, Fire Department, and local Poison Control Center, along with a neighbor's number, should be readily available and posted on or near the telephone.

2. Lifeline services can save valuable time, especially with a caregiver present. Help is just a press of a button away. The service will quickly send the most appropriate assistance and will notify you about what actions were taken. (1-888-767-5583)

3. Place cordless phones around the home for increased accessibility in an emergency.

4. Fill out a "File for Life" or "Vial for Life" medical information card. (Described in previous section.) These cards can be obtained through your local Fire Department. If your district does not have a "File for Life" program, call a district next to yours to see if they have it. These files contain all pertinent medical information a paramedic could use in helping treat a loved one in an emergency. The information is magnetized to the refrigerator or put in a medication looking bottle that goes in the freezer.

5. Consider Residential Knox Box – this is a lock box (like Real Estate agents use) that attaches to the front door and allows only the Fire Department to get in without having to break down the door in an emergency. The price of these is $139-176. Call your local Fire Department for more information.

GENERAL SAFETY

6. Test smoke alarms and carbon monoxide detectors regularly.

7. Install night lights for safe movement at night.

8. Secure all throw rugs in place to keep them from slipping.

9. Avoid throw rugs and scatter mats in high traffic areas.

10. Clear high traffic areas of obstacles making it easier to maneuver.

STAIR SAFETY

11. Install additional stair railings. Two railings are better than just one.

12. Consider converting a living room on the first floor into a bedroom to avoid stair climbing.

13. Make stairwells well lit.

14. Clear stairs of clutter.

15. Wear reading glasses when stair climbing.

16. Demonstrate to the caregiver how the patient goes up and down the stairs.

BEDROOM SAFETY

17. Install a light switch at the entrance to the bedroom.

18. Consider side rails for a bed to facilitate ease in getting up.

19. Position the bed against the wall and use guardrails on the open side. In the absence of guardrails, have the caregiver position the wheelchair alongside the bed as a barrier.

20. Have a bedside commode available to decrease the distance and time traveled to and from the bathroom.

21. Teach a family member and the caregiver on proper bed positioning to reduce pressure and prevent skin breakdown (for bed bound elderly).

22. Install a baby monitor to alert the caregiver of immediate needs.

23. Provide a clear path from bedroom to bathroom.

BATHROOM SAFETY

24. Install grab bars in the shower/tub area to assist with transferring in and out.

25. Consider a tub transfer bench to help with getting in and out of the bathtub. (Medicare does not pay for a tub bench or tub transfer bench.)

26. If stepping over the tub is safe, using a plastic lawn chair that has arm rests works great while using a hand held shower head.

27. Install a grab bar next to the toilet to help with getting up.

28. A raised toilet seat will help in getting up and down.

29. Medicare will cover the cost of a bedside commode. It can be converted to fit over the toilet, and will avoid an out-of-pocket expense for a raised toilet seat.

30. Place non-skid mats on the bathroom floor and in the

bathtub to prevent slipping.

KITCHEN SAFETY

31. We recommend that the caregiver cooks a family member a light meal to demonstrate

accurate use of stove, microwave, and appliances.

32. Be sure there is a fire extinguisher located in the kitchen.

33. Make oven mitts handy for the caregiver to use.

MOBILITY IN LIVING AREAS

34. Measure doorways for a wheelchair, and make any adjustments possible.

35. Install ramp to get in and out of the house if needed.

36. Consider replacing that favorite recliner with a lift chair. Another option would be to attach blocks or a platform underneath the chair to raise the height. This will make it much easier to get up for people with arthritis.

37. Be sure that any device used to assist with maneuvering around the house is safe. This includes all furniture, appliances, doorways, etc. Some things can move unexpectedly causing a fall.

38. Rearrange furniture to provide adequate room to maneuver with a wheelchair or walker.

39. If you are having trouble with any of these areas, consider getting a doctor's order for a home care physical therapist to come out for a Home Safety Evaluation.

CLOTHING:

Regardless of our age or physical condition, we want to look and feel our best. Today's clothes options make that a much easier goal to reach. When buying clothing for your Senior consider:

40. Clothing that is washable and wrinkle-free.

41. Slacks and skirts that have elasticized waistbands are easier to get on and off.

42. Socks with non-skid tread on the bottom.

43. A long arm shoehorn.

44. A hand held "clothes reacher" to pick-up clothes.

45. If the patient and caregiver are having difficulty with dressing and bathing, consider getting a doctor's order for Occupational Therapy Evaluation.

MEALS:

46. As people age, their taste buds diminish. This changes their appetite and desire for food. Chewing and swallowing may also be a challenge. As these things develop, contact

your doctor about evaluations with nutrition and speech/language professionals.

47. Your family member may need to be on a pureed diet and/or thickened liquids to prevent swallowing challenges.

EXERCISE:

48. Create a home exercise program in consultation with your family member, caregiver, physician, physical therapist and occupational therapist.

A good home exercise program designed by a physical therapist can improve:
- Circulation (blood flow)
- Reduce swelling in ankles
- Improve lung and heart function
- Help with posture
- Mental alertness

DAILY ROUTINE
A well-planned routine can make the more demanding parts of the day go more smoothly, for both your Senior and their caregiver.

Make a list that consists of:

49. Likes and dislike of food. Write down favorite recipes.

50. Times medications are to be taken (with or without food).

51. Any favorite TV shows that are a must see. (The Price is Right or Soap Opera.)

52. How the patient likes their coffee or tea made.

53. Medical restrictions of sweets or salt.

54. Favorite games (card or board or other).

55. Favorite topics of conversation.

OPTIONS TO CONSIDER PRIOR TO GETTING A CAREGIVER

56. Lifeline (This is the "I've fallen and cannot get up" button pendant that a senior wears around their neck or on their wrist that they can press to alert paramedics.)

57. Home Video Surveillance

58. Several companies now sell digital devices sets for the entire family. Some allow family members to monitor each other's vital data.

When Your Parent Should No Longer Be Driving

Do you remember when you got your driver's license? Your world became much bigger the moment the examiner handed you your new license. It was a big step in gaining freedom and independence.

For many Seniors, giving up their driving rights can be a stressful experience.

There can be many reasons a Senior should no longer be driving.

For examples, side effects from medications, impaired vision, or memory loss.

If your Senior is still driving, regularly inspect the car to look for scratches, scrapes or dents. Ride with the Senior to evaluate their driving abilities.

If you determine that your Senior is becoming a hazard to him/herself, or to other drivers on the road, then hopefully, you can simply have a heart-to-heart talk about your concerns, and you can mutually decide when it's time for your Senior to stop driving.

But what if your Senior isn't ready to turn over their keys?

Suggest a driving test.

Whether they get tested at your local Department of Motor Vehicles, or possibly through your insurance company, it might be an easier decision if this kind of formal evaluation indicates they are no longer safe to drive.

A few ideas to make the transition easier:

- Come up with a transportation plan, so your Senior doesn't feel he/she has lost his/her independence.

- Planning consistent days each week for grocery shopping, trips to the pharmacy, shopping, etc. can help with their transition.

- There are also many options for transportation through public and private services.

- Some home caregivers may also be willing to provide some transportation.

- You give permission to the caregiver to drive your Senior's vehicle, and add the caregiver to their insurance policy as an additional driver.

- Other possible transportation options: Medivan, Uber, taxis, public transportation options, and private companies. (Do a google search for "transportation for seniors" in your area.)

Different Types of Services to Help Your Parent Stay in their Home (or Yours!):

<u>The Senior moves-in with one of their adult children or another relative.</u>

You might determine that it would be best for your Senior to move in with you, one of your siblings or another relative or close friend.

It will be important to do an evaluation of your home to determine any alterations or safety precautions that need to be added.

For example, adding railings in the bathtub or shower to prevent falls, or converting a room on the main floor into your Senior's bedroom so they don't have to go up-and-down the stairs.

In my "checklist packet," available for downloading at **SafeatHomeHealthCare.com**, you can go through each room in your home to evaluate any alterations you need to make to keep your Senior safe.

Often in this type of situation, a family will still use the services of a home care agency, especially if they work during the day.

You could also consider looking at Adult Day Care programs. Do an online search for "Adult Day Care" (or contact my team and me, through my website).

Costs typically range, depending on services provided, between $65 to $90 per day, including lunch. Some offer pickup/drop-off services, too..

Depending on your Senior's policy, these costs may be covered by their long term care insurance policy, too.

The Senior remains in their home, using Home Care services:

Using services of a home care agency are perfect if your senior is still capable of living on their own, but starts to need some assistance with common tasks, such as light house work, laundry, or errands.

Depending on both their physical health, and their mental acuity, they might also need any range of personal care services including bathing, dressing, taking medications, issues with incontinence, and meal preparation.

If you choose a reputable, well-run agency, home care services will be provided by well-trained, compassionate individuals.

Their time can vary from a few hours of assistance per day, to 24-hour service.

My team of mentors and I want to make sure you find the best agency, and choose the best level of care for your Senior's needs, your family's needs, and your Senior's financial situation.

Go to **SafeatHomeHealthCare.com** for a **FREE** consultation.

We are committed to helping Seniors and their families make good decisions to provide the very best care for Seniors.

The Senior remains in their own home, with Home Health Care service:

Perfect for the independent Senior, who has health issues that require assistance and monitoring by a licensed health care professional.

It could be a nurse who monitors their blood and vital signs regularly. Or, your Senior might be recovering from some type of health episode or surgery, and needs physical therapy for a period of time.

Typically these services are "prescribed" by the Senior's doctor, and that way, costs can be covered through Medicare.

If you have any questions about the steps you need to take to get Home Health Care services started for your Senior, again - my team of mentors and I would like to help. Schedule a connection by going to our website: **SafeatHomeHealthCare.com**.

Geriatric Care Management

A Geriatric Care Manager (GCM) is a licensed medical professional (typically a nurse) who is hired by a family to manage the Senior's care.

Usually, I see GCM's hired when the Senior's adult children live out-of-town, and they want to make sure their Senior is getting the very best care and attention.

As I explained in a previous section, a Geriatric Care Manager is often given Power of Attorney and control of the Senior's financial management, in addition to making decisions about home care and home health care services.

Because of the costs involved, these services are mostly used by high net worth families.

One advantage is the Geriatric Care Manager will have access to all of your Senior's medical information. The GCM will also be monitoring your Senior frequently and can provide feedback to the family.

Examples

My home care agency, Safe at Home Health Care, recently provided home care services for the Dad. His son is not a good planner, and not comfortable with making decisions about his Dad's care.

They hired a Geriatric Care Manager.

She arranges things such as doctor and dentist appointments, she frequently checks on Dad (even though he has fabulous home caregivers), and she follow-up after his doctor visits to implement any new instructions from the doctor.

I would also recommend a GCM for a family that has many adult children.

Bernice, another client my agency assisted with home care, had six adult children. She lived in a farmhouse, and had sold the land surrounding the house, which brought in several million dollars to the family.

The six kids fought all the time. Unfortunately they wanted to come to Mom's house and argue about the money in front of Bernice.

Because she had dementia, and truly disliked all of their arguments; she would agree with whichever son or daughter was in the room at the time.

The Geriatric Care Manager can take an objective, non-emotional view. They are a liaison that can help orchestrate the care plan and many other services for a senior.

Part IV: When it's Time to Move Your Parent to a Facility

Assisted Living

Another alternative is Assisted Living.

Often it becomes difficult for your Senior to do the maintenance and upkeep at their home. Everything from mowing the lawn, changing filters, or shoveling snow from driveways and sidewalks often has to be done by you.

Suddenly you find yourself doing all the maintenance for two homes — yours and theirs —and it's chewing up a lot of your time.

It's also a good choice when one of your parents has passed, and Mom or Dad is now living alone.

Assisted living facilities are perfect for the active, social Senior, since they typically have scheduled activities daily.

There are many options available. Typically the Senior will have their own apartment, but several services are provided such as meals, administering medications, laundry, errands, and regular activities.

This can be a way for your Senior to stay active and connect with others their age.

Nursing Home Care

If your loved one needs daily medical care, a nursing home is the best option to provide daily medical care and provide 24 hour monitoring.

When they no longer need day-to-day medical care (perhaps they were in the nursing home for rehab, after a surgery or event such as a stroke), the Senior might be able to return home.

Some Seniors would prefer to be at home with hospice services, when they are nearing the end of their life.

When your Senior is in either an assisted living facility, or nursing home care, it's important to make frequent visits and at varying times.

First, to be frank, this gives you an opportunity to monitor the care your Senior is receiving, without being predictable.

I don't mean to sound pessimistic here, because the majority of both assisted living and nursing homes provide excellent service.

Even so - the best way to monitor the care your Senior is receiving is by being unpredictable and frequent with your visiting times.

Also, Seniors suffering with dementia often experience what is known as "sundowners." They're great in the morning hours, but around 4pm, their dementia worsens and they might be missing the dinner meal and medications.

You also want to be actively involved in the decision making, when a nursing home increases the level of care (and in turn, the costs) for your Senior's care.

For example, for a Senior who is in "memory care" services in a nursing home, there are three different levels of service.

The facility should have specific guidelines for determining which level they are providing, and what determines increasing that service level.

Ask for specific details, and know the rules in your state.

If you have concerns about any of the services your Senior is receiving, address them with the Director of Nursing immediately.

This should be documented, and you should request a copy.

You also want to scrutinize every single bill, and, if your Senior has long term care insurance, review them with the Senior's insurance agent to ensure everything possible is being covered, either by their long term care insurance, or supplemental health care insurance.

Don't hesitate to schedule an appointment with the facility's billing department to review every single charge.

Nursing home costs add up quickly, and you need to manage these expenses well.

The bottom line is you need to continue to be the advocate for your Seniors - no matter where they are living.

Part V: The Final Days

The Final Stage - Hospice

There are many reasons to use Hospice care.

For example, maybe your Senior's health has continued to decline, and it's clear they are nearing the end of their life.

Or treatments and medications that are intended to prolong the Senior's life are no longer working, and they are suffering and in tremendous pain.

Your Senior might be battling a life-threatening illness, such as cancer, and their prognosis is not good.

Here's a couple important questions to discuss, both as a family and with your Senior's doctors:

What is the prognosis – the expected course – of my family member's illness?

What are the goals for care? For instance, is the goal to cure the disease or to provide comfort and improve the quality of my family member's life?

Hospice or Palliative Care can be provided by compassionate, well-trained individuals who focus on making them comfortable.

It's intended to maintain the quality of life for your loved one.

Some families choose hospice service in their own homes. Others receive hospice care in a Nursing Home or other facility.

Hospice care does not speed up or slow down the dying process. It provides support to both the Senior and the family, and also assists with coordinating services (for example, contacting the mortuary) after your Senior has passed.

What to Do When Your Senior Passes

You and your Senior planned well. You helped your Senior - your Mom or Dad, or perhaps a Grandparent - live their best life possible, all the way to their final days.

After you've had the opportunity to say your final goodbyes, it's time to let the professionals do their work.

If your Senior passes away while living in an assisted living or nursing home, the facility will contact your chosen mortuary to safely transport them to the funeral home.

The same is true if your Senior has passed away at home, under hospice care. The Hospice Nurse will handle all the details of legally pronouncing your Senior's death, and contacting the mortician.

If your Senior passes away at your home, while under your care, call 911 to ask for the assistance of a coroner. They will come to your home to certify that your Senior has passed, and assist with contacting the funeral home to transport your Senior's body.

You'll need to contact your Senior's elder law attorney, and the funeral home director. But if your Senior completed the pre-planning I described earlier — most of the work has already been done.

I've included a helpful **post-life checklist** in the package you can download for FREE by going to: **SafeatHomeHealthCare.com.**

Celebration of their Life

You've been so helpful in your parent's final years.

It's difficult to lose a loved one, but at the same time, you can have the peace of mind knowing that you helped your Mom or Dad, or other relative, live their life to the fullest during the final years.

Celebrate their life. Share great memories and stories. Put together a picture slideshow. Think about how much they helped and influenced your life.

No matter what your religious beliefs - celebrate your Senior's life as they requested.

Grieving Support

Everyone handles grief differently - and that includes how long a person grieves.

Losing a loved one - especially a parent - can be difficult.

I want to encourage you to reach out for help and support as you go through the grieving process.

There are many resources through hospice services, churches, even health or mental health professionals.

Asking for help when you're having difficulties dealing with this type of loss is one of the best things you can do for yourself and your family.

Part VI: How Can I Help?

Many thanks to all the incredible Seniors, and their families, that I've been able to assist through my home care agency — Safe at Home Health Care.

I'm grateful every day that my team of caregivers, mentors, and I have been able to provide help and support to make life better, easier, and safer for your Seniors during their final years.

I've attended many of my client's funerals, and here's my observation.

Families who manage the last years of their Mom or Dad's lives well, celebrate their lives without regret.

If your family is dealing with taking care of aging parents, in the very best way possible - my team and I would love to help.

Go to my website: **SafeatHomeHealthCare.com** or call us at 630-465-0481.

RESOURCES

For Families:

Download my "Checklist Packet" for lists and evaluations mentioned throughout the book by going to: **SafeatHomeHealthCare.com.**

You will also find quizzes and other helpful information. I also recommend subscribing to my email list to receive regular tips for keeping your Senior safe.

For Compassionate Individuals Who Would Like to Learn More about Being a Home Care Mentor:

You don't have to be a licensed health care professional to help seniors. My special "Home Care Mentor" program will teach you how to identify families who need assistance, assist with pre-screening, and connect them to the best home care agencies to fit their needs.

Learn more by going to: HomeCareMentors.com

For Agencies

I'm passionate about helping families and their Seniors, so I offer complimentary training to help agencies improve their services, attract and retain top quality caregivers, and provide the very best service for their clients.

Go to: HomeCareEntrepreneurs.com to learn more.

For Experts:

Are you a Home Care Agency, an Elder Law Attorney, a Financial Planner, a Geriatric Care Manager, a Physician, or a Mortician?

Learn how you can use this book as a resource for your own clients.

Go to: HomeCareEntrepreneurs.com

About the Author

Kurt Hjelle is passionate about helping Seniors and their families as they deal with managing a Senior's care in their final years in life.

He's an entrepreneur and expert in home health care services, and his company is completely changing the face of the home care services industry.

By developing his ingenious "Home Care Mentor" system, Kurt ensures that all participants in an elderly person's care are working as a team. In fact, his system guarantees it.

His special program helps:

- elderly individuals in need of home care services
- the sons and/or daughters of the elderly individual who need help navigating through the home care provider selection process
- the small agencies who are so swamped juggling home care providers' schedules, and dealing with mounds of government paperwork, that it's difficult to both market their services and stay closely connected to their clients
- home caregivers who are eager for and well-prepared for assignments, and at times, need some coaching and assistance while dealing with their elderly customers

Kurt has a simple mission: **Help Others.**

Go to: **SafeatHomeHealthCare.com** for more information or email kurt@safeathomehealthcare.com, 630-465-0481.

Finding Experts in Your Area:

Look inside the back cover of this book for experts in your area;

OR

Go to: SafeatHomeHealthCare.com to schedule a FREE consultation.

Made in the USA
Middletown, DE
11 February 2022